York
Pocket Guide

Ian Sampson

Colin Baxter Photography Limited, Grantown-on-Spey, Scotland

First published in Great Britain in 1997 by
Colin Baxter Photography Ltd, Grantown-on-Spey, Moray, Scotland

A CIP catalogue record for this book is available from the British Library
ISBN 1 900455 19 6

Printed in Hong Kong

York
Pocket Guide

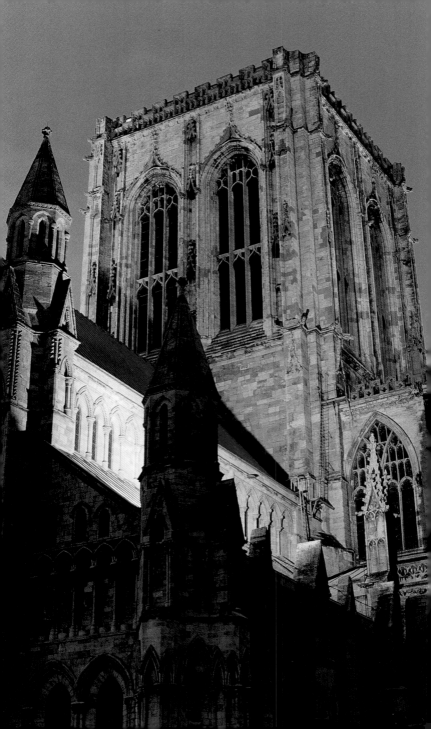

INTRODUCTION

A Visitor's Introduction

York caters well for its many visitors. Introductions to the city are available in a range of interesting and varied ways: (1) a guidebook (2) an exhibition (3) a guided tour – on foot, by bus, by horse-drawn carriage and on a river cruise along the Ouse.

Up-to-date information is always accessible to visitors from one of the Tourist Information Centres and first-time visitors will need a street map of the city (provided in this Pocket Guide and also available in other guidebooks and as a folded sheet).

(1) A guidebook. This Pocket Guide offers a quick and easy reference to over 70 places of historical and modern attraction. They are located on the six pages of street maps in the Guide.

(2) An exhibition. Amost all the exhibitions in the city's museums and historic buildings provide an insight into the history of York. The most notable of these are the world famous Jorvik Viking Museum (see p.49), York Castle Museum (see p.44) and the Yorkshire Museum (see p.54).

(3) A guided tour. Visitors are welcome to enjoy a free guided tour around historic York in the company of a trained voluntary guide, starting from Exhibition Square each day (April-Oct). A private tour company also provides a number of daily walking tours starting from the West End of York Minster. There is also the opportunity to hire a personal stereo and headphone set; the tape gives a commentary on two walking routes around the city. Tours by open-top bus take about an hour and include a commentary on all the main sites of interest. A pleasing tour at an easy pace is available from the seat of a horse-drawn carriage. Seeing the city from a different perspective can be enjoyed by a river cruise along the Ouse.

The Essential York

At first, the choice seems a little overwhelming. One thing is almost certain, most visitors will leave York hoping to come back another day to see all the delights that they never had time to visit.

Surely no-one would want to miss the jewel in the crown – York Minster. That apart, the short walk along the city walls between Bootham Bar and Monk Bar will be memorable, as are the views from the tops of York Minster's tower and Clifford's Tower. Some experiences are unavoidable and the delights of an ancient city pervade

York's narrow streets and even narrower 'snickelways'. Visitors should include at least one historic building and one medieval church during their time in the city. Personal interests will determine which of the many museums visitors decide to explore but whenever there is need for a breath of fresh air then a relaxing stroll through the Museum Gardens or Dean's Park will revive the mind and body. Don't forget that like many great cities, York has a river – many a foot-weary soul may be refreshed by a cruise along the Ouse.

City of Glass

York has been called the 'City of Glass' for it has one of the finest collections of medieval stained glass in the world. There are almost 200 such windows among the city's parish churches, historic buildings and the Minster. These magnificent windows have survived throughout the centuries; only the thin channelled lead strips need replacing every 100-150 years. The traditional skills required for the maintenance and repair of stained glass are still practised by the York Glaziers' Trust. A pair of binoculars provides the best means of appreciating the intricate work involved in creating these transparent treasures.

Streets, Snickleways & Bridges

More than one stranger to York has noted that this is a city where the streets are called 'gates' (eg. Micklegate); the gateways are called 'bars' (eg. Bootham Bar); and the bars are called pubs. The name of a street can sometimes be traced to an earlier age and may be a personal name (Goodramgate comes from Gutherum, a Danish chief) or a trade (Coppergate was Danish for the street of the coopers or barrel makers and woodworkers).

The suffix 'gate' is used in many city street names, reflecting the Danish influence. The word 'gate' comes from the Danish word 'gata' or 'gatan' for street or way. York has a profusion of narrow alleyways, ginnels, passageways and snickets threading their way through the city, many of which date from medieval times. The word coined by the author Mark Jones in his best-selling book on these many footways in York is 'snickelways'.

For over a thousand years (850-1863) there was but a single road bridge, the Ouse Bridge, across the river. Lendal (1863) and Skeldergate (1882) Bridges alleviated the situation and eased the flow of traffic in and out of the heart of the city. Taking a leisurely stroll around the city streets and snickelways can provide an absorbing interest for resident and visitor alike.

Festivals and Events

York has a full programme of festivals and events, details of which are published each year and available from the Tourist Information Centres. The York Early Music Festival in June has gained international acclaim and the Viking Festival braves the February weather with a longships regatta, torchlit procession, boat burning and fireworks finale. York's Cycle of Mystery Plays are performed every four years. Racing enthuisiasts will need no introduction to the the Knavesmire which provides one of the highlights of the horse-racing social calender – the Ebor Meeting in August. Regular horse-racing meetings were first held in York during the 18th century .

Night-time

Evening entertainments are provided at York's two theatres, cinemas, night clubs and the York Barbican Centre. There are night-time cruises on the river and the boats are equipped with powerful on-board floodlights which illuminate many of York's famous buildings and land-marks. York is one of the most densely haunted cities in England and there are chilling tales of disembodied spirits which are recounted on the many ghosts walks which take place each evening throughout the year. At night, street lighting adds drama to a stroll through familiar street scenes and many of the city's notable buildings are floodlit.

River Ouse

The River Ouse is something of an exception – it does not have its own headwaters or source. Instead, it is born some 10 miles (16 km) north-west of York at a point where the River Ouse is joined by a small stream called Ouse Gill Beck. The combined waters are then re-named the River Ouse.All of the Yorkshire rivers which flow into the Vale of York are collected by the Ouse which takes a meandering 57 miles (92 km) to join the Humber, east of Goole, and then continues to the North Sea.

In terms of the development of a city, the River Ouse is one of England's most important rivers. From AD 71 when the Romans chose to build their fortress at Eboracum (York) between the confluence of the Ouse and the Foss, the River Ouse has been a central feature in the story of the city. Invading armies sailed up the river, including the Vikings and the Danes. Stone to build the city's magnificent medieval cathedral, York Minster, was brought from Tadcaster during the 11th century via the Wharfe and the Ouse. And it was the river which provided the vital ingredient in the development of a thriving and prosperous inland city throughout the medieval period.

MULBERRY
HALL

THE STORY OF YORK

The history of England from AD 43 to 1066 is a tangled web of stories which records a series of invading armies, most of whom came to conquer and stay. They each stamped some of their own cultural identity upon the villages, towns, cities, countryside and people of England. At almost every turn on a saunter through the streets of York there is some reminder of the rich tapestry woven by 2000 years of human occupation. Traces remain of the successive waves of Romans, Angles, Saxons, Vikings and Normans who sailed across the sea from their European homeland. They all made York their prized possession of the north. As George VI observed in his often-quoted words, 'The story of York is the story of England'.

The Romans

During the first century AD the spread of the Roman Empire across Europe seemed unstoppable. The invasion and occupation of Britain began in AD 43 with the landing of troops in southern England. Under instruction to quell a warlike confederation of tribes known as the Brigantes in northern England, the soldiers of the Ninth Legion marched from Lincoln into Yorkshire and chose a site near the confluence of the River Ouse and its tributary the River Foss for their new command post.

Starting in AD 71, the Roman army set about building their new fortress which they named Eboracum (York, as it is known today). A large rectangular site of 50 acres (20 ha) was surrounded by a broad ditch and high banks of earth topped with a stockade of wooden fencing. Situated halfway along each of the four sides was an entrance gateway. By Roman law, civilians were not allowed to live in the fortress

Opposite: Mulberry Hall, Stonegate.

9

so a thriving town gradually spread outward from the walls.

The site of the main gate (Porta Praetoria) lies beneath St Helen's Square and faced a bridge over the River Ouse. Troops entering this gateway continued down the street (Via Praetoria) which is now the route of Stonegate. It led to an intersection with their principal street (Via Principalis), now underlying Petergate. Nearby this intersection was the commander's headquarters – the site now occupied by York Minster. Part of it was revealed when excavations took place to strengthen the Minster's foundations and can be seen in the Minster's Undercroft Museum.

From about AD 107, strengthening of the defences by stone gateways and stone walls began a continuing programme which included rebuilding work in about AD 200 and again around AD 300. The stone was transported by ship on a river journey of about 15 miles (24 km), via the Wharfe and the Ouse, from quarries near Tadcaster.

The Ninth Legion departed from York in about AD 120 and was replaced by the Sixth Legion. The numbers of professional Roman soldiers in Eboracum rose to over 5000 men. One of Eboracum's most important characters was Constantine the Great (AD 274-337) who was also the founder of Constantinople. On the death of his father (Constantius Chlorus, Caesar of the West) in Eboracum in AD 306, Constantine was proclaimed joint Emperor of the Roman Empire by his troops. That such an appointment could have been made here in Eboracum shows the importance of both the city and the man, already a renowned soldier. It was thanks to Constantine that Christianity was proclaimed as a permitted religion under Roman law in 313. He is to be honoured with a bronze statue which will be erected outside the south door of York Minster – close to where his statue originally stood at the commander's headquarters in Eboracum.

With the steady decline of the Roman empire, the Roman army was recalled from Britain in the early 5th century. In Eboracum as elsewhere in England, their military and civilian services were brought to an end. Nevertheless, the fortress walls continued to be the main means of defence as the city changed from the control of the Romans to new foreign invaders – the Anglians (7th century) and the Vikings (9th century).

There is now very little to see of Eboracum or its stonework. However, the ruined south-west corner tower (the Multangular Tower) of the fortress wall is the city's best surviving example of Roman stonework. It can be seen in the Museum Gardens.

The Name 'York'

It was quite usual for the first-century Roman invaders to adapt the existing name of a British settlement and provide a latinised version. When the Romans arrived in AD 71 at the site of their proposed new fortress in Yorkshire, a small Brigantian settlement already existed near to the confluence of the Ouse and Foss. The Brigantes called it Eburacon. Using an obvious adaption, the Romans called their fortress by the almost identical name of Eboracum. In both languages, the interpretation of this name is taken as 'the place belonging to Eburos' or 'the place where the yew trees grow'.

The Romans chose a boar as the emblem for their fortress town and this remained the town's emblem under the Anglo-Saxons, who decided to use their own word for a boar (eovorwic or eoforwic) for the name of the town. It continued as Eoforwic until another wave of invaders, the Vikings, took over in the 9th century. The name of a town often changes its spelling when translated from one language to another, in order to accommodate the ease of pronunciation. Whatever Eoforwic sounded like to the Vikings, they wrote it down as Jorvik. To the English, this is pronounced more easily as York.

Angles, Saxons and Vikings

The vacuum left by the Romans was filled by invaders from the contintent of Europe. Successive waves of Angles and Saxons, tribes of Germanic people, sailed across the sea and took control. The Anglo-Saxon way of life was established. King Edwin's acceptance of the Christian religion in 627 saw the dawn of a new era of enlightenment and peace; the first York Minster was built and in 735 the Pope granted York the pall of an archbishop. But life in York was to take yet another change in the 9th century – Scandinavian seafarers were on the horizon. Raiding and pillaging by hordes of Vikings culminated in a battle at York in 867. The victorious Vikings established a new kingdom, ruled from their thriving city of Jorvik.

Medieval York

The last successful invasion of England was in 1066. William the Conqueror divided the newly conquered country among his Norman barons and together they set about establishing their authority and power. Things did not run smoothly at first in York due to rebellion against the new Norman overlords and incursions along the Ouse by marauding Danes.

William's solution included a garrison of troops, the construction of two wooden castles (York Castle and Old Baile) and the extension of the fortified area of the city with lines of earth ramparts. This incorporated two sides of the original Roman wall and increased the protected area of the city to about five times the size of the Roman fortress. Only one of the Roman gateways (Bootham Bar) was used in the revised fortifications.

On the spiritual side of life, the Norman overlords gave encouragement to the setting up of monastic institutions throughout England and the construction of St Mary's Abbey was begun in York in 1088.

The Norman earth mounds formed the foundation on which the medieval city walls were built some 200 years later. The money to build the walls during the 13th and 14th centuries was raised from a new tax called murage (muri in Latin means walls) which was imposed on all goods entering the city.

At over two miles (3.2 km) in length, the curtain walls were a notable defence, constructed with four main bars (entrance gateways), six posterns (lesser gateways) and 37 interval towers. Each of the four bars had a portcullis (substantial trellised oak gate with iron spikes) and a barbican (extension archway with another gateway). The posterns had a tower and an arched gateway at the side of the tower.

The Bar Walls of York are the finest remaining circuit of medieval city walls in England and one of York's prime attractions, available to visitors free of charge.

York prospered during the Middle Ages and became a bustling river port. Its medieval guilds built their own halls, three of which

Part of the 13th-century stonework of St Mary's Abbey. After it was closed by the Dissolution in 1539, the abbey was pillaged for its stone and left in ruins.

survive to this day. Each craft, controlled by its guild company, contributed its own play to the Mystery Plays which were performed round the city. The skill acquired by an apprentice was called 'the mystery', hence the popular name given to the plays.

The Royal Connection: King Richard II created the royal connection by conferring the first title of the Duke of York upon his uncle, Edmund de Langley, on August 6, 1385. Edmund was the fifth son of the previous monarch, King Edward II, and since the 17th century, most English monarchs have given their second son the title Duke of York. (Prince Andrew, second son of Queen Elizabeth, is the 14th duke to hold the title). King Richard also fell out with his London administration and took his royal court to York on March 24, 1396.

For a time, York vied with London to be England's capital city. York was given a new charter with extended powers, privileges and the title of 'the county of the city of York'. In the 17th century, York featured once again as the royal capital when Charles I moved his court here for six months at the start of the English Civil War in 1642.

Victorian York

George Stephenson has been crowned the 'Father of the Railways' but it was another George, a York man, George Hudson, whose energy and business acumen gained him the title of 'The Railway King.' This linen draper of humble origin exploded on to the scene in the midst of 19th-century railway mania and in blunt Yorkshire fashion gave the oft-quoted promise that he would 'Mak' all t'railways cum t'York.'

Britain's main line railway network (some

13,000 miles, 20,920 km) was built with great speed between 1830 and 1870. This great Victorian railway-building boom stimulated unprecedented growth in the economy with its demand for iron rails and building materials in particular. George Hudson headed his first railway company in 1835 and soon became the most influential man in 19th-century York, directing an ever-expanding empire of railway companies.

Over-zealous and unscrupulous dealings led to George Hudson's downfall and disgrace. He was removed from office in 1849. At that time, over a quarter of the lines built in Britain were controlled by Hudson's inter-connected companies. He achieved a dream but lost an empire. His legacy to the city, however, could scarcely be over-stated but the scandal of his dishonest conduct resulted in the hatred of his name in York.

A telling symbol of York's illustrious railway history is the impressive station. The original station was built in 1841 within the medieval walls, but proved to be too small for the city's burgeoning business in railways. When the new station opened in 1877 it was the largest in the country. It has since been extended several times, but remains one of Britain's finest examples of Victorian railway architecture. The Royal Station Hotel (now called the Royal York Hotel) was opened in 1878 alongside the new station.

York did indeed become the railway capital of the North on the main line between London and Edinburgh, playing a major role in the national network and establishing a key centre of administration. For a time, it could also claim to have one of the most important carriage-building centres in Britain. The National Railway Museum is housed in York, within walking distance of the city centre.

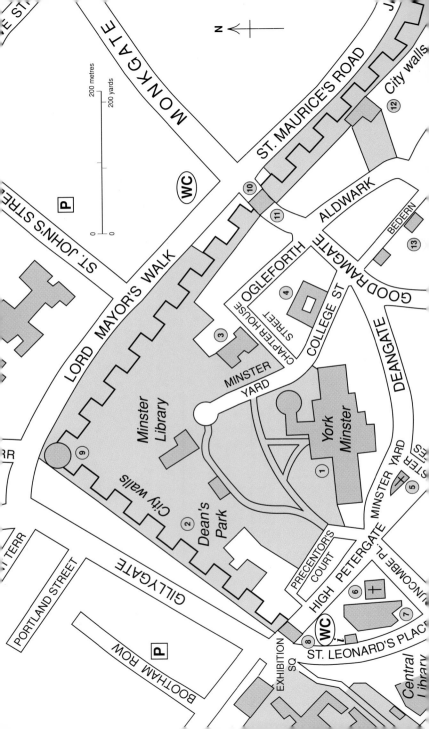

YORK MINSTER & ENVIRONS

York's magnificent cathedral is the building of prime interest for almost all first-time visitors to the city. However, other riches are close by; a popular section of the medieval city walls lies here with notable gateways, there are medieval buildings and guildhalls, an elegant town house with the finest furnishings, a theatre and a pleasant green parkland in which to wander in peace and tranquillity.

(1) **York Minster:** Christianity gained freedom from its early persecution by the Romans in 313, under the Edict of Milan. The proclamation was issued jointly in the names of Constantine the Great and his brother-in-law Licinius, and granted the freedom of worship throughout the Roman Empire. In 314, Bishop Eborious of Eboracum (York) is recorded as being one of three British bishops who attended the Council of Arles in France, but there is no indication of the site of his church in York.

In the 7th century, King Edwin (616-32) of Northumbria embraced the Christian religion and a small wooden church named St Peter the Apostle was hurriedly built in his capital city Eoforwic (York) for his baptism by Bishop Paulinus on Easter Day, 627. Although humble in construction, this place of worship was the seat of the bishop; it contained his throne (cathedra) and therefore had the status of a cathedral and the main church in the diocese. This was the first York Minster. From about 670 work began on re-building the cathedral in stone and the 7th century York Minster served the city for some 350 years, surviving through the capture and occupation of the city by the Vikings from 867 onwards. But disaster struck in 1069.

After the Norman Conquest of England in 1066, a troop of Norman soldiers was sent to occupy the city of York. In 1069, under severe attack from a combined force of northern rebels and Danes, the Norman garrison set fire to some buildings near to the Minster in order to keep the invaders at bay. Sadly, the flames spread and the Minster was destroyed in the fire. Thereafter the story of the Minster is one of rebuilding and reconstruction. The present magnificent Gothic cathedral was begun in

Looking over Dean's Park towards York Minster, from the Bar Walls.

1220 and took 252 years to build.

The word 'minster' originally described a church or mission centre which was served by a group of clergy, ministering to the surrounding area. Although its full title is 'The Church and Metropolitan Cathedral of St Peter in York', the cathedral is best known as York Minster.

A view of the towering strength and beauty of the West Front of the Minster lifts the eye through an array of soaring buttresses, carved niches and traceried windows to the top of its elegant, eight-pinnacled twin towers. This world-famous cathedral abounds with evidence of the skilled craftsmanship and dedication of the medieval age in its intricate stonework, delicate woodcarvings and wealth of medieval stained glass.

The main visitor entrance into the Minster is through a side door at the West End which leads into the nave. This is the main body of the church where the congregation sit; a line of seven pillars separates the nave from its side

aisles. High above are the wooden ribs of the ceiling with carved wooden 'bosses' at the intersections.

Standing at the 'crossing' immediately below the central tower, there is a view of two very important stained-glass windows. In the north transept wall is the largest 13th-century window in the world with five very tall window openings – the Five Sisters Window. High on the south transept wall is The Rose Window with a ring of 24 outer panels containing red roses alternating with white on red roses, symbolising the union of the Houses of Lancaster (red roses) and York (white roses).

The South Transept of York Minster in the glow of a winter sunset. The Rose Window is set high in its gable end. Both the transept roof and the window were restored after a fire in 1984.

From the crossing, pass through the imposing choir screen directly into the area of the choir. Stone carved figures of 15 Kings of England (William I to Henry VI) stand within the recesses of the choir screen.

Carved wooden seats, known as stalls, provide seating for the clergy and choir. All cathedrals have a special throne, a 'cathedra', for their bishop. In the case of York it is the seat of the Archbishop of York.

At the east end of the Minster, behind the choir, is one of the cathedral's greatest treasures – The Great East Window. It holds the world's largest area of medieval stained glass in a single window.

Further delights await those who visit the octagonal Chapter House, the Undercroft Museum and climb the steps of the Tower. Conducted tours are given by the Minster Guides and there is a wide range of souvenirs and books available in the Bookshop.

Dean's Park: The parkland around part of ②
York Minster is open to the public. You can enter through the gate by the West Front of the Minster or from the cobbled Minster Yard. A tree-lined path curves round past the Minster Library, which was originally the 13th-century chapel of the Archbishop's Palace (now no longer standing).

Treasurer's House (Minster Yard): A world ③
of 17th and 18th century elegance abounds in this magnificent town house, situated within the shadow of York Minster. In medieval times there was a house on this site which belonged to the treasurer of York Minster but only part of the original house remains.

The office of treasurer was made redundant in 1547 after the Dissolution of the Monasteries (1536-40) and the present property was built on the site in the 17th century. Due to enlargement over the centuries and re-styling with Dutch gabling it is a mix of various architectural styles. In 1720 the house was divided; the old part, now called Gray's Court, was restored and is used by the University College of Ripon and York St John.

The chief interest in the Treasurer's House lies with a rich eccentric, Frank Green, who bought it in 1897 and set about a three-year programme of radical reconstruction with the

celebrated York architect, Temple Moore. Inside there are some real treasures, including a mock medieval hall with half-timbered gallery, Flemish tapestries, floor-to-ceiling panelling, Venetian chandeliers, and ornate lavatories. Tranquillity reigns in the walled garden and there is a licensed tearoom, exhibitions, gallery shop and a programme of events.

Chapter House Street: Immediately to the northeast of the Minster lies this narrow, cobbled street. It overlies, in part, the route of the Via Decumana which led into the heart of the Roman fortress from one of the four entrance gates. The route was probably a

Treasurer's House. An intriguing history of ownership and architecture surrounds one of York's most interesting houses. In the 1960s a Roman road was discovered beneath the cellar floor.

constant source of irritation to the medieval clergy who would no doubt object to a noisy thoroughfare disturbing the peace of their Cathedral Close. Eventually the original Roman gateway was blocked and a new entrance (Monk Bar) was built around 1330 guarding Goodramgate.

St William's College (College Street): This ④ timbered 15th-century building, close to York

The front of St William's College is part of the original 15th-century building. Above the doorway is the figure of St William, a 12th-century Archbishop of York.

Minster, was originally a college and home for the chantry priests (clergy who were employed to say continual masses for the donor of an altar or chapel) of the Minster. After the Dissolution of the Monasteries (1536-40) the college was sold, eventually becoming a rather run-down collection of private dwellings. Its former glory was restored in the early part of this century and now houses 'The World of the Minster' Museum. Three medieval halls are open to visitors provided that they are not in use for functions and there is also a restaurant and shop.

St Michael le Belfrey (Minster Yard): A ⑤

16th-century church which is now administered from St Cuthbert's Church, Peasholme Green. Guy Fawkes was baptised here.

Petergate: Originally the route of the Principal Way (Via Principalis) of the Roman fortress, High and Low Petergate stretch from Bootham Bar to King's Square. This major city street takes its name from the dedication of York Minster to St. Peter. Note: (i) No. 25, Young's Hotel, claims to be the birthplace of Guy Fawkes (he also lived for a time in a house in Stonegate). (ii) Firemarks, these are plaques which were placed on the front of a building at first storey level. They indicated that the property was insured against fire by one of the insurance companies which operated their own private fire brigades during the 18th and 19th centuries; (iii) Cigar Store Indian, the American Indian with his brightly painted headgear once drew the attention of customers to a tobacconist.

Precentor's Court: Graceful houses border this peaceful, narrow, early 17th-century street which concentrates the mind on the majesty of York Minster with its 200 ft (61 m) tall pinnacles towering into the heavens above.

Duncombe Place: A wide street which provides a famous view of the West Front of York Minster. It was created in the 1870s by enlarging a narrow lane and then re-named after Dean Duncombe who persuaded the Council to undertake the construction and made a private subscription himself.

⑥ **St Wilfrid's Church** (Duncombe Place): Built in 1864 in Victorian Gothic style. Daily services are held in the church and the times are given on the entrance notice board.

⑦ **York Theatre Royal** (St Leonard's Place): York's oldest theatre; it maintains an enviable reputation for its programme of repertory theatre and touring productions.

Bootham Bar: One of the four major bars (8) (gateways), built of stone in medieval times, Bootham Bar is the only bar which used the site of an earlier entrance to the Roman fortress of Eboracum. It guarded the north-west entrance to the medieval city and parts of the stonework are 12th century. Although the city council resolved to demolish the bar in 1832, it was saved by a public outcry and

Three stone statues survey the scene from the top of Bootham Bar, against the familiar backdrop of York Minster.

in the end, only the barbican (a pair of outer walls with a gateway) was pulled down.

Note the two upper storeys (14th century); the side arches (19th century) and the three stone statues on top of the bar (a lord mayor, a knight and a mason – carved in 1894). Climb the steps at the side of the bar; on the first floor there is an imposing portcullis.

Bootham Bar is the best place to start a walk of the Bar Walls and the section to Monk Bar has impressive views over Dean's Park and towards York Minster.

Robin Hood's Tower: This corner tower is (9) met on the walk along the city wall between

Bootham Bar and Monk Bar, but does not have any outer access. There are some fine views from here into Dean's Park; the large, red brick building is the Deanery, home of the Dean of York.

10. **Monk Bar:** This gateway, thought to be the finest, was built in 1330 and was originally called Monkgate Bar in reference to a monastery which was located in the vicinity. A top storey was added in the 15th century and although the barbican was demolished in 1825, Monk Bar remains the tallest and most strongly fortified of the four main bars and its portcullis is still in working order. From the top-most turrets of the bar you will see the six stone-carved figures who are at the ready to hurl missiles upon the approaching enemy.

11. **Richard III Museum** (Monk Bar): Be the judge in the reconstructed modern-day 'trial' of this much-maligned English king who held the throne for less than two years (1483-85). Is the portrayal of him as an evil hunchback true – or was he a fair and courageous monarch?

12. **Merchant Taylors' Hall** (Aldwark): Originally built in the 14th century by the honourary members of a religious order; it was taken over in the 15th century by the Company of Merchant Taylors, one of the York guilds, as their guildhall. The outer cladding is 17th century but there is a fine medieval roof over the main hall, and panelled walls and some notable windows in the Council or Counting Hall.

13. **Bedern Hall** (off Goodramgate): Between 1979 and 1980, York City Council restored the basic shell of a 14th-century building. The hall was originally part of an extensive range of buildings which formed the college of the Vicars-Choral (choristers and servants at York Minster). Funds were raised by three of York's guilds to reconstruct a medieval guild hall.

THE CITY CENTRE

York is a very compact city. Centred around the old market place of St Sampson's Square there is an intriguing web of interconnecting streets and 'snickelways' which spread out to reach the city walls. Streets, both broad and narrow, threading through the city centre, are thronged with shoppers and sight-seers during the busy summer season. From tiny-roomed retail outlets (some housed in the oldest row of properties in the city) to large department stores, there is an abundance of choice in the thriving city-centre shopping areas.

Looking down on the cluster of buildings either side of Stonegate, with St Helen's Square and the Mansion House at top right.

In the heart of the city a sense of history is never far away. There is a wonderul mix of shops, restaurants, cafes, and tea rooms. The list of historical places to visit includes delightful medieval churches such as Holy Trinity, Goodramgate and the fantasy of medieval timber construction displayed in the Merchant Adventurers' Hall.

14 **Judges' Lodging** (Lendal): The bust on the front of the building is Aesculapius, the Greek god of medicine, and is a clue to the fact that the property was built in the early 18th century by an eminent York physician, Dr Wintringham. From 1806 to 1976 the residence was used by the Assize Court judges on

their attendance at the York Court. It is now a hotel.

Guildhall (St Helen's Square): To reach the ⑮ Guildhall, visitors must walk through the archway at the side of the Mansion House. The 'tie bars' above the passageway were used for hanging meat, keeping it 'fresh' in the breeze!

The Guildhall was the meeting place for all the York guilds who were responsible for

On the east bank of the River Ouse is the 15th-century Guildhall, seen here from Lendal Bridge.

running the city. Bags of gold arrived here in 1647 from London after the end of the Civil War (1642-46) and £200,000 in gold pieces was placed under guard until it was counted and handed over to the Scots whose army had been hired by the victorious Parliamentarians under Cromwell.

The original 15th-century hall was a casualty of a World War II bombing raid on 29th April 1942. Almost totally destroyed, the full restoration was finally completed in 1960 and it now houses the local government adminstrative centre for the City of York Council.

(16) **Mansion House** (St Helen's Square): The city of York provides this fine building as a private home for its Lord Mayor during his or her term of office. This is the only 'city hall' in England which is used in such a way. Designed by Lord Burlington and built in 1725-30, the Mansion House is more than 20 years older than its counterpart in London. Both the dining room and state room have authentic Georgian furnishings.

The ancient title of Lord Mayor was conferred upon the Chief Magistrate of York by Richard II in 1392. Although many cities throughout England have a Lord Mayor, only in London and York does the Lord Mayor have the right to use the prefix 'The Right Honourable'.

This elegant house is a private home and is not normally open to the public but an application for a visit may be made by writing to the Civic Secretary, Mansion House, York YO1 1QL.

Mansion House in St Helen's Square. Since the early 18th century, York has provided this fine house for its Lord Mayors to use as a private home whilst in office.

(17) **St Martin le Grand** (Coney Street): A small chapel in this busy thoroughfare offers some welcome peace and quiet. Only part of the original medieval church still stands; it was another of the city's casualties during the World War II bombing raid of 1942. The south aisle was eventually reconstructed and the remainder made into a paved garden. Thankfully the notable 15th-century window,

one of the finest in the country, can still be admired (it had been removed for safety, prior to the bombing). Visitors can hardly miss the huge replica of a 17th-century ornate clock which projects out from the church and over the pavement – it looks like a giant pocket watch. On top is the Little Admiral, an affectionate name given to the small figure of an 18th-century naval officer reading his sextant. When first constructed, the figure used to rotate with his sextant, following the sun.

Unfortunately, during the World War II air raid the mechanism was ruined. The gilded head of Father Time can be seen set against the side of the clock. The Little Admiral, apart from his mechanism, survived the air raid fire but the original 17th-century clock and Father Time did not and were replaced.

The church clock of St Martin le Grand, projecting high above pedestrians in Coney Street. The Little Admiral on top of the clock has stood here since 1778.

Coney Street: A busy shopping street which takes its name from the Danish 'Konung' for king. Originally called King's Street because it led northward to the 11th-century palace of the famous Danish Earl Siward who died in Jorvik (York) in 1055.

St Michael's Church (Spurriergate): With a religious heritage spanning eight hundred years, this church is now a Christian Centre serving refreshments, selling fair-traded goods and offering a listening ear to anyone troubled by the demands of life. The 12th-century arcades are a remarkable feature of the interior, in addition to the wonderful 15th-century glass.

Coppergate: The Danish origin of the name signifies that it was the street of the woodworkers. Leading off Coppergate is Coppergate Walk. It was underneath this pedestrian precinct and adjoining shops that the great excavation took place which revealed the streets of Jorvik and the vast array of Viking

artefacts from the 9th and 10th centuries.

Pavement: The city of York has yet another strange name for a street. In 1086 it was recorded as Market-shire but was re-named Pavement as it most likely was the first street in the city to be paved. It was presumably widened at the same time.

Public executions took place here in Pavement, the most notable being that of Thomas Percy, 7th Earl of Northumberland, who was engaged in the Catholic rising of 1572. Note: Sir Thomas Herbert's House: look above the shoe shop and admire the imposing period facade of this 16th-century house.

Sir Thomas Herbert's House, Pavement. Sir Thomas, who was born here in 1606, became an adviser and close friend of King Charles I. The house was bought and restored by the York Civic Society and is now a shoe shop.

All Saints' Church, Pavement (Situated ⑲ between High Ousegate and Coppergate): Despite its popular designation, All Saints' is not actually in Pavement. The church was originally much closer to the junction of all the converging streets, including Pavement, before the start of street widening and the demolition of parts of the church from the 17th century onwards.

From the outside there is a view of the fine octagonal lantern tower, rebuilt in 1837; the upper storey windows were designed to let light spread down into the central part of the church. In medieval times, a lamp was hung within the lantern tower and it provided a guiding beacon of light across the dense Forest of Galtres (north of the city) for the benefit of travellers.

This church was, and still is, closely associated with the commercial

The octagonal lantern of All Saints' Church, Pavement dominates a part of the city centre skyline. Added in the 15th century and rebuilt in 1837, the lantern is still illuminated each evening from dusk.

life of the city; inside are the shields of the city's guilds. The strange 13th-century door knocker on the north door, referred to as the Doom Knocker (or the Mouth of Hell), is said to depict a beast swallowing a human being.

Merchant Adventurers' Hall (Piccadilly ⑳ and Fossgate): This property is a prime example of York's rich heritage of medieval buildings. Of the three parts (undercroft, chapel and Great Hall) the most memorable is the exquisite fantasy of timber construction to be seen in the Great Hall with its eight bays and two massive spans. Adjoining the hall is the chapel with its original wooden screen. In the undercroft are the oak pillars which support the structure of the building above. Here is a timbered tribute to 14th-century design, skill and craftsmanship; there will be few surviving medieval guildhalls in the whole of Europe to match this Great Hall, the largest timber-framed building in York. For 600 years, the trade in 'goods bought and sold foreign' in York were controlled by the Company of Merchant Adventurers. This group of merchants who ventured their money in foreign trade formed the most powerful and wealthiest medieval guild in the city. Their guildhall had space for charity – the undercroft was a hospital for poor people and had cubicles where the guild's

pensioners could live; worship – they held services in the chapel; and business, meetings and feastings, in the Great Hall.

Whip-ma-whop-ma-gate: Connecting Colliergate with Pavement, this has the double distinction of being the shortest street in York and the street with the longest name. Although popularly interpreted to mean the place where miscreants were whipped, some suggest the original medieval name of 'Whit-Nour-What-Nour-Gate' roughly translates as

Coat of Arms over the entrance, from Fossgate, to the Merchant Adventurers' Hall. Founded in 1357, the Company of Merchant Adventurers was the most powerful medieval guild in York.

33

'Call-That-A-Street-You-Must-Be-Joking!'

The ARC (St Saviour's Church, St ㉑ Saviourgate): Within the walls of a carefully restored medieval church, visitors get a hands-on experience of the past. At the Archaeological Resource Centre there is a chance for everyone, whatever their age, to be something of an archaeologist. What secrets do some of these ancient relics hold? Visitors can find out how computers are used in archaeological investigation and discover the crafts of yesteryear.

The Shambles – one of the most famous and best-preserved medieval streets in Europe.

Shambles: Leading from King's Square to Pavement, this is York's most famous, narrow street where some of the overhanging upper storey of the timber-framed buildings lean unsteadily towards each other. Recorded in the Domesday Book of 1086, the street was rebuilt in the late 14th century and many of the present buildings date from between 1350 and 1475.

This street became a centre of trade for the city's butchers and along the front of some shops are the large heavy shelves, called shammels, which were originally used for the display of meat. At least the tall overhanging buildings would have kept the meat in the shade and relatively cool. It was the shammels which gave rise to the street name of The Fleshammels (the street of the butchers) and this was eventually shortened to The Shambles. Note: (i) The shammels and meat hooks. (ii) No. 35: St Margaret's shrine. Margaret Clitherow, the young wife of a butcher, was martyred in 1586 for the unlawful hiding of a Catholic priest. This was a time of religious persecution of the Catholics in England under a ruling Protestant monarchy (Elizabeth I) and for her act of treason,

SCARBOR'O FISH AT IT'S BEST

Margaret Clitherow was put under a door and crushed to death by a huge weight of stones heaped on top. Margaret was canonized (declared a saint) in 1970. Although No. 35 is the official shrine, further research suggests that her actual residence may have been opposite, at No. 10.

22   **Newgate Market** (between Parliament Street and the Shambles): An open-air market which has a wide range of stalls with fresh foods, clothing, gifts and household items.

   King's Square: This was the site of one of the four Roman gateways to the fortress Eboracum and led into the street called Via

During medieval times York had a prosperous open-air market which served a large surrounding area of countryside. Now in Newgate Market, the stalls sell a wide range of goods including fresh fish from Scarborough.

Praetoria (now Petergate). The square takes its name from the fact that the Viking kings made their palace here.

St Sampson's Church (Church Street): This church has been restored and converted into a day centre for senior citizens. St Sampson was a British monk who became a Bishop of Brittany in the sixth century.

St Sampson's Square: For more than six

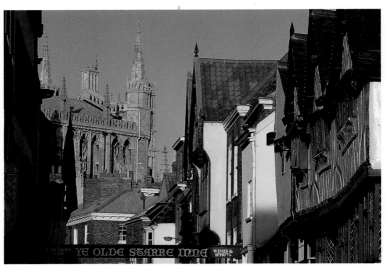

In Stonegate, the painted beam which advertises Ye Olde Starre Inn is the only surviving sign of its type (a 'gallows' sign) in the city of York.

centuries this was the centre of an open-air market in the city and the area was known as 'Thursday Market'. The market was moved into its larger neighbour, Parliament Street, in 1835 and Thursday Market was given its new name in 1841.

Roman Bath (St Sampson's Square): Inside the pub called 'The Roman Bath' there is a view, thanks to the ingenious use of mirrors, into the underground excavation of a vast, stone-built installation where the Roman soldiers enjoyed a relaxing bath. The Romans had an extensive sewer system running through the fortress.

St Helen's Square: The site of one of the four Roman gateways. Known as the Praetorian Gate and built about AD 300, it was the chief entrance into the fortress. It was later the site of the graveyard for St Helen's Church.

㉕　**St Helen's Church** (St Helen's Square): This ancient church, restored several times and partially rebuilt, dates from the 14th century. The medieval glass painters used it as their Guild Church and many of the craftsmen's names are recorded on a plaque at the west end of the church. Today it serves as York's civic church, and special services attended by the Lord Mayor and Council Members are held here.

㉖　**Assembly Rooms** (Blake Street): During the second half of the 17th century, York became the centre of social life for the well-bred and wealthy families of the north of England. It made a welcome alternative to the tedious journey to London. A building was required in York to match the style of living of its fashionable patrons. This is it: Georgian elegance at its very best and one of the finest buildings of the period in England, designed by Colen Campbell on the commission of Lord Burlington. First used in August 1732 and completed in 1735, its impressive interior received the northern nobility and landed gentry

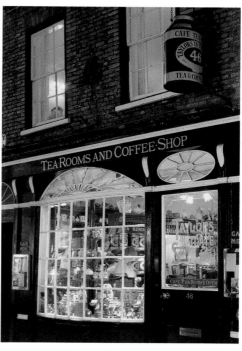

Continuing the tradition of fine tearooms and coffee houses in York is the famous Taylors Tearooms and Coffee Shop in Stonegate.

who danced and gamed their hours away in opulent style. The ladies had one criticism – the interior columns were too close to permit the easy passage of their hooped skirts. The 18th-century ballroom makes a splendid setting for a cafe-restaurant.

Stonegate: The street overlies the route of the Praetorian Way (Via Praetoria), one of the two principal intersecting streets of the Roman fortress, Eboracum. When the Minster was being built, the massive stones were brought by cart along here from the riverside wharf near the Guildhall. Twenty thousand tons of stone were required for the central tower alone, so there is little surprise that it became known as Stonegate. Today the street is paved with York sandstone.

The earliest known printer's press was established in the street

The Red Devil, famous York landmark, sits above a former printer's home in Stonegate.

in about 1500 and from then on Stonegate became renowned for its printers, publishers and bookshops.

Stonegate is a famous shopping street, and provides many tantalising glimpses of the Minster, framed by the city buildings. For centuries the street has enjoyed a vibrant commercial life and the intriguing mixture of architectural styles evoke an unmistakable link with the past. Note: (i) No. 10, a beautiful example of the tilers' craft, a Minton tiled fascia.

(ii) Mulberry Hall, which dates from 1434. (iii) No. 13, Stonegate's naked lady – the figurehead of a late 17th-century trading ship. (iv) 'Ye Olde Starre Inne' is one of the oldest pubs in York with its coaching signboard. Close by, don't miss the narrow passage or snicket leading into Coffee Yard. (v) No. 33, under the eaves of a former printer's home squats the Red Devil, one of the most photographed figures in the city. Although not proven, he is reputedly a 'printer's devil'. The little 'devil' in question was the nickname given to a printer's apprentice whose duty it was to carry the hot type in a print shop. (vi) A large Bible hanging from above the doorway at No 35 signifies that this was at one time a bookshop. (vii) By No. 52 with the signboard to Stonegate Gallery: a narrow alley leads to the remains of the oldest dwelling house in York dating from the 12th century.

On the corner of Minster Gates and High Petergate is a seated statue of the Goddess of Wisdom. The Romans called her Minerva (as she is known here); the Greeks named her Athena.

Minster Gates: A narrow footstreet leading from the south end of York Minster to the junction of Stonegate with Petergate. This was the centre of the Roman fortress and also the cross-roads of the two main Roman streets (Via Principalis and Via Praetoria). The finely preserved, seated figure of Minerva, the Goddess of Wisdom, with books and a wise old owl, can be seen high above a bookshop at the junction of Minster Gates and Petergate, looking down Stonegate. Before the Minster was completed, the street was called Bookbinders' Alley and Minerva's presence is a reminder of the importance of books.

Coffee Yard: An ancient, dog-leg passage, very narrow in places. Tall people are warned to look out for low overhead beams. A truly intriguing passageway which links Stonegate

A wet night in Grape Lane. This is one of the oldest, and shortest, streets in the city. York's first coffee house stood on the corner of Grape Lane and Coffee Yard.

(entrance near 'Ye Olde Starre Inn' signboard) with the junction of Swinegate and Grape Lane. The printers, publishers and booksellers of 18th-century York would meet here in a coffee house, hence the name. Centre of conversation, communication and steeped in printing history, York's first newspaper appeared in 1719 from a printer in Coffee Yard. Note: Thomas Gent's Coffee House (17th century).

Barley Hall (Coffee Yard, via Swinegate or ㉗ Stonegate): In the 14th century a townhouse was built here which was under the ownership of Nostell Priory, near Wakefield. In the 15th century it became the residence of a properous goldsmith and alderman of the city.

The interior of a house originally built in the 1480s is carefully reconstructed in this handsome timber-framed property which is named after the late Professor Maurice Barley, first chairman of the York Archaeological Trust which was formed in 1972.

Goodramgate: A street with a name of

Danish origin (Gutherum is thought to have been a Danish chief). Our Lady Row, a terrace of characterful properties, is the oldest row of houses in York, dating from 1316. They are now a selection of small, quaint shops.

28 **Holy Trinity Church** (Goodramgate): Another peaceful gem in the city centre. An interesting church with a rare pitched roof (a saddleback), 15th-century glass, 18th-century box pews and a two-decker pulpit. The oblong opening in the side chapel, known as a squint or hagioscope, allows a view of the high altar during mass. Access is through the archway and iron gate at one end of Our Lady Row.

Holy Trinity Church stands in a quiet corner, screened from view by the shops and houses of Goodramgate. The East Window of this medieval church is a rare example of 15th-century stained glass.

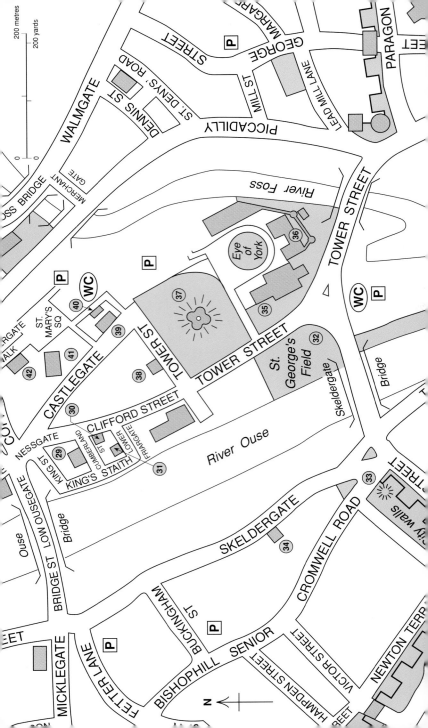

SOUTH OF THE CITY CENTRE

In the southern part of the city is a peninsula of land which is bounded by the easy flowing waters of the River Ouse and its tributary the River Foss. Their confluence can be reached by the riverside walkway which leads from the southern end of St George's Field car park.

This part of the city has a wealth of places of interest for the visitor. There are no fewer then seven museums including the world-famous York Castle Museum, an 18th-century townhouse which is one of England's finest and Clifford's Tower, the only remaining part of York's 12th-century castle.

29 **Grand Opera House** (Cumberland Street): A superbly restored Edwardian theatre which presents a full programme of family entertainment including national touring shows, plays, musicals, ballet and pantomime.

30 **York Dungeon** (12 Clifford Street): Don't be afraid to scream (there are many who do) in what is described as a perfectly 'horrible' experience. Unbelievably evil villains, horrific torture and murder are all part of human history. Hopefully, visitors will survive the bloody history which is revealed. (This exhibition is not for those of a nervous disposition, nor for very young children).

31 **Friargate Wax Museum** (Lower Friargate): Definitely something different. Beware of nooks and crannies, someone will be there. Heroes and villains from books and films are here in attention-holding sets as well as a chamber of horrors (the Black Cave) and a portrayal of England's colourful history and heritage.

32 **St George's Field** (Tower Street): An area of parkland.

33 **Baile Hill** (Cromwell Road): William the Conqueror built a wooden castle keep (Baile

Castle) on the summit of the large artificial mound in 1086. Along with its twin (York Castle, now Clifford's Tower) they provided a defence of the city from both banks of the Ouse. The mound, Baile Hill, was planted with trees in 1722 and at the base there is a small 19th-century tower.

Yorvik Brass-Rubbing Centre (57 ㉞ Skeldergate): This is one place where no experience or expertise with coloured waxes is required in order to reproduce the wonderful illustrations which are found in English church brasses.

Eye of York: Name given to the circle of grass which lies between Clifford's Tower and the York Castle Museum. In the 11th century it lay within the walls of the castle built by William the Conqueror.

Crown Court (Eye of York): This fine 18th- ㉟ century court building was designed by the York architect John Carr in 1770. The Female Prison (1780), directly opposite (now part of York Castle Museum), has an almost identical facade. It was also Carr's work.

York Castle Museum (Eye of York): ㊱ Famous throughout the world for its much-photographed cobbled Victorian street, this is England's largest and most popular folk museum which is housed in two former prisons – the Debtors' Prison (1705) and the Female Prison (1780) – now linked by a modern concourse.

The museum owes much to the inexhaustible enthusiasm of Dr Kirk, who came from the Yorkshire market town of Pickering. He offered his amazing private collection of items from the past to York City Council. In 1938 they let him design his own museum in the former Female Prison. Appropriately called Kirkgate, the famous re-creation of a Victorian cobbled street in the old exercise yard was Dr Kirk's own idea. The hansom cab waits for a fare but is not available for hire. There is a whole street of shops which provide continual interest to window-shoppers.

The museum was a great success and expanded to fill the nearby Debtors' Prison which was originally built in 1701. It was here that Dick Turpin spent the last three months of his life and his cell is on view, as empty as when he left for his execution on 7th April

1739. In the prison yard is another street re-creation, Half-Moon Court, this time with the re-building of a variety of shops which existed in the heart of the city from around 1900 to 1914. Allow up to two hours to visit this absorbing museum.

Clifford's Tower (Tower Street): There are 55 steps to climb up the mound and a further ascent to the top of the tower to reach the tower-top walkway and some outstanding views of the city. A wooden castle (Baile Castle, 1068) and its twin (York Castle, 1069) were built on opposite banks of the Ouse to defend the city by William the Conqueror. In 1190 the

Two of York's former prisons, both built in the 18th century, have been transformed into the country's most popular folk museum – the York Castle Museum. It includes a re-creation of a Victorian cobbled street.

city's Jews took refuge in the castle keep from a local violent mob. Offered Christian baptism or death, they chose mass suicide. The wooden tower was burnt to the ground.

The tower is the only remaining part (the keep) of the 13th-century York Castle which was constructed in stone on the mound of William's castle. The Cliffords were one of the major land-owning families in the north of

Clifford's Tower stands on top of a huge earth mound. The mound was originally built on the orders of William the Conqueror in 1069 and had a wooden castle set on top. The present stonework dates from the 13th century.

England throughout the medieval age and there are at least two associations which connect the name of Clifford with the tower. Sir Roger Clifford fought on the losing side at the Battle of Boroughbridge in 1322 in which the arch-enemy of the crown, Earl Thomas of Lancaster, was soundly beaten and King Edward II regained complete control over his kingdom. After the battle, Sir Roger's body was brought to York and hanged in chains on the tower. Secondly, a number of Cliffords were appointed to the position of constable of York castle from the 14th century onwards.

Regimental Museum (Tower Street): Three

hundred years of military history is on display. The men, the regalia and the story of the wars that were fought through the centuries are revealed. The silver and brassware treasures of the Royal Dragoon Guards and the Prince of Wales' Own Regiment of Yorkshire are among the many magnificent military items on view.

㊴ **Fairfax House** (Castlegate): Perfect symmetry without and perfect elegance within,

Fairfax House is undoubtedly the finest Georgian townhouse in York and stands as a masterpiece among England's 18th century architecture. It takes its name from Viscount Fairfax who moved from London to York in the late 1750s and commissioned the building of the house for his only surviving daughter Anne, perhaps thinking of it as a dowry.

John Carr of York was the architect. He also designed the famous Yorkshire stately home of Harewood House, acquired a national reputation and was at one time Lord Mayor of York. No expense was spared; the finest craftsmen were employed including Joseph Cortese, an

From the top of Clifford's Tower there is a fine view across the rooftops of York. The steeple of St Mary's Church, Castlegate, the highest in the city, is on the left here, with the Minster in the distance.

Italian, who created the superb plasterwork ceilings. The same high standards were achieved in the carved woodwork and the ironwork.

Sadly the magnificent home suffered both neglect and misuse over the following centuries. In the 1920s the owners of the neighbouring St George's Hall Cinema bought Fairfax House and turned the first floor into a

Fairfax House was built in the middle of the 18th Century and is perhaps the finest example of a period-furnished Georgian townhouse in England.

dance hall. Despite a number of insensitive treatments of such a rare treasure, there was no irretrievable damage.

In the 1980s, Fairfax House passed into the caring hands of the York Civic Trust; the purchase price was paid by the National Heritage Memorial Fund and a remarkable collection of Georgian furniture (The Noel Terry collection) was given to the Trust. The glories of the original Georgian era were lovingly restored for everyone to enjoy. Today's visitor will find an overwhelming experience of 18th century gracious living amidst a superbly decorated interior and the collection of elegant furniture.

㊵   **Impressions Gallery** (29 Castlegate): A major photographic gallery with innovative exhibitions, popular talks, workshops and a renowned specialist photographic bookshop.

㊶   **York Story** (Castlegate): A converted church, St Mary's, which has the tallest steeple in York, is used as an exhibition centre. There are plans to change the exhibition but it currently provides an audio-visual presentation which recounts the 1900 years of York's history from Roman to modern times and gives an ideal introduction to the city. The present exhibition has some marvellous collections, panoramic murals and models, including a striking display where the sculptured medieval builders are seen at work among their rudimentary scaffolding of wooden poles and woven platforms. Details of the changes at this exhibition centre are available from the Tourist Information Centres.

㊷   **Jorvik Viking Centre** (Coppergate Walk): Deep underground, a time-car takes visitors on a journey back through the past thousand years. Transported slowly through a Viking street, visitors are then surrounded by the sights, sounds and smells of an ancient city built by the people who sailed across the sea and conquered the capital of the North in the 9th century. They called their city Jorvik.

Not only is there a wonderful re-creation of Viking life but the timber walls of their houses can be seen exactly where they were discovered by the archaeologists who dug deep beneath the city streets. Well preserved in the water-logged soil were the remains of a whole community, their houses, workshops and all their worldly goods. Hidden for a thousand years, the world of the Vikings is now revealed. It was first uncovered in 1976. Under the busy thoroughfare of Coppergate, the world's time-clock has stopped at the year 948.

0   200 metres

0   200 yards

N

BOOTHAM

BOOTHAM ROW

P

. MARY'S

ST. MARY'S LANE

MARYGATE

YGATE

43

EXHIBITIC
SQ

ST. LEONAR

48

47

44

Museum

Gardens

45

46

*Central
Library*

Observatory

49

50

River Ouse

WC

Lendal Tower

MUSEUM STRE

ndal

LE

EXHIBITION SQUARE & MUSEUM GARDENS

Within the Museum Gardens is the oldest substantial piece of stonework in the city of York. Known as The Multangular Tower, it dates from the days of the Roman fortress in the 4th century.

Also within the grounds of the 10-acre (4 ha) park are the Yorkshire Museum (containing some of Europe's rarest archaeological treasures) and the 13th-century ruins of St Mary's Abbey along with its gatehouse and hospitium.

Before taking a stroll through the gardens, many visitors will be interested to note the history of King's Manor (see p 52) and the displays which are offered in the city's art gallery.

Exhibition Square: Items to note include The De Grey Rooms built in 1841-2 and named after Earl De Grey, primarily to provide an officers' Mess of the Yorkshire Hussars. One of York's Tourist Information Centres is now housed in this building.

The statue is of William Etty, the renowned York artist whose work is exhibited in the Gallery. At his feet is a model of Bootham Bar which he and others campaigned fiercely to preserve after the city council had resolved to pull down the walls and bars.

43   **York City Art Gallery** (Exhibition Square): The Gallery was built in 1879 as an exhibition centre for the Yorkshire Fine Art & Industrial Institution. In addition to its renowned collection of Old Masters, the exhibition covers the last 600 years of European painting and a collection of British paintings from the 16th to the 20th century with fine water-colours, drawings and prints of York. The statue outside is of William Etty, R.A. who was born in York in 1787. In the gallery there is a

comprehensive display of his work. Regarded by many at the time as disreputable because of his nude paintings, the art world has since paid tribute to his talent. There is a programme of temporary exhibitions, lectures, recitals and other events at the gallery.

King's Manor (off Exhibition Square): A  house, sometimes referred to as the Abbot's Lodgings, was originally built here in the 15th century as the home of the abbot of nearby St Mary's Abbey. However, the abbot's house was taken over when the abbey was dissolved in 1539 during the Dissolution of the Monasteries (1536-40) by Henry VIII. On Henry's orders, the abbot's house became the official residence and headquarters of the Lord President of the King's Council of the North, hence the popular name for the property. The Council was a kind of northern Parliament which continued here, in York, until the Council was abolished in 1641.

Above the entrance to King's Manor is the imposing Royal Coat of Arms of King Charles I (1625-49). The lion and unicorn support the crosses of England and Scotland respectively.

Anne Boleyn, who had a tragically brief marriage (1533-36) to Henry VIII, is said to have stayed in York at the Abbot's Lodgings. After the dissolution of the abbey, extensive alterations were made to the abbot's house and the property soon became a fit place in which to provide hospitality for visiting royalty. Henry himself resided at King's Manor with his fifth wife, Catherine Howard, in 1541. Later monarchs included James VI of Scotland whilst on his journey to London, to be crowned James I of England & Scotland, in 1603 and then again in 1617. Charles I also stayed here fives times between 1633 and 1642 when York was a Royalist stronghold.

The visits of James VI and Charles I are commemorated with a carving of their initials at King's Manor. On the base of the uprights either side of the main entrance are the initials JR (Jacobus Rex). Above the door, on the Royal Arms, are the intials CR (Carolus Rex). The lion supports the Cross of England and the unicorn supports the Cross of St Andrew for Scotland. At the end of the building, left of the main doorway, is a small window (by reputation the smallest window in York). It dates from around 1480 and looked out from a garderobe (lavatory).

During the English Civil War (1642-44) the city of York changed control from the Royalists to the Parliamentarians and back again during 1644 in some bloody skirmishes, one of which took place around King's Manor. With such a chequered career it is little wonder that there are no less than three tales of ghostly manifestations which haunt this historic building. The first is a phantom monk who wanders peaceably among the buildings of the former Abbot's Lodgings. Perhaps the apparition of a gentle lady in a green Tudor costume, carrying a bunch of roses is the ghost of Anne Boleyn whose soul carries happy memories of York. The final tale is far from pleasant. Echoing around the main courtyard fom time to time are the harrowing cries and of the wounded Parliamentarian soldiers who were brought here for primitive medical treatment during the battles for the city in 1644.

After the Civil War, King's Manor was

occupied by private tenants and later divided into apartments. From 1883, the building became the Yorkshire School for the Blind. Today, King's Manor belongs to the University of York which has its main building in the village of Heslington about a mile south-east of the city.

Museum Gardens (entrances from Museum Street and Marygate): Visitors may stroll, sit, picnic and enjoy the tranquillity of this delightful city park which covers ten acres. Within the grounds are the Yorkshire Museum, the Museum Botanical Gardens, the ruins of St Mary's Abbey, the Hospitium, the abbey gatehouse, the Multangular Tower, part of the original Abbey Walls and the York Observatory.

Yorkshire Museum (Museum Gardens): Some of the rarest archaeological treasures in the whole of Europe can be seen in the Yorkshire Museum which stands within the ten acres of the Museum Gardens. It houses some of the greatest finds of past ages in Britain from Roman, Anglo-Saxon, Viking and Medieval times, including The Middleham Jewel, an exquisite 15th-century gold pendant adorned with a magnificent sapphire. This was found in 1985 near Middleham Castle.

In addition to its displays of Yorkshire wildlife, special events and lectures, the Museum has stunning new exhibitions presented in the most entertaining fashion and draws visitors from far and wide.

St Mary's Abbey (Museum Gardens): Evocative ruins of the 13th-century abbey church add a sense of history to a stroll through the Museum Gardens. Monastic life began here in 1088 when a group of Benedictine monks was granted a site for a new monastery. For a time it was the richest and most powerful abbey (a large monastery) in the north of England and belonged to the Benedictine order. Ruined in a fire, the abbey was rebuilt in 1270 and destroyed yet again, along with all other English monasteries, by Henry VIII in his Dissolution of the Monasteries (1536-40). All that remains are the ruined abbey church, the Hospitium near the river and the 15th-century gatehouse

④⑧   **St Olave's Church** (Marygate): St Olave

refers to Olaf, a king of Norway who was killed in battle in 1030. He was canonised in 1164 and made the patron saint of Norway, hence the church flies the Norwegian flag. A medieval coffin lid indicates the early foundation of this site. The present church is mainly an 18th-century rebuilding after being badly damaged during the English Civil War (1642-46) when the tower was used as a gun platform. The tomb of the York artist William Etty (1787-1849) is in the churchyard.

When the **Observatory** was completed in 1832 it housed the largest telescope in the world and was one of the country's finest

St Mary's Abbey. Its extensive grounds are now known as the Museum Gardens. When it closed in 1539, St Mary's was the third largest abbey in England. The abbey church was about two-thirds the length of the present York Minster.

55

observatories. The conical roof was designed as a revolving structure by John Smeaton who was noted for his design of the third Eddystone Lighthouse which was eventually dismantled and re-erected on Plymouth Hoe. Thomas Cook of York built the observatory.

Hospitium (Museum Gardens): The attrac-  tive medieval Hospitium with its stone-built ground floor and a timbered upper storey was part of a group of buildings belonging to St Mary's Abbey and was used as a guesthouse for the abbey's visitors.

Multangular Tower (Museum Gardens): Multangular means 'many angles' and the tower has 14 sides, nine of which project into the Museum Gardens. The lower section of this unique tower is the oldest substantial piece of stonework to be seen in the city and

The Multangular Tower, the lower section of which is the city's best surviving example of stonework from the Roman period. It dates from the time of Emperor Constantine in the 4th century.

formed the south-west corner tower of the Roman fortress built about AD 300. From the inside of the tower, visitors can see the Roman walling which is built to a height of 19 ft (6.2 m).

When the city walls were rebuilt and extended in the 13th century, the Roman corner tower was heightened (note the larger stones). The stonemason's plaque mistakenly describes this as the NW Tower (it is the SW Tower).

Lendal Tower (Lendal Bridge): Standing on the left bank (inner city side) of the River Ouse at Lendal Bridge is a notable stone-built tower known as Lendal Tower or St Leonard's Tower. It was originally built as one of the city's medieval defence towers and resembled its much-lower, opposite number (a watch tower now known as North Street Postern Tower) on the other side of the river. As there was no

bridge across the river at this time, a ferry operated between the towers until 1863 when Lendal Bridge was built.

In the 17th century, stone was taken from the ruins of St Mary's Abbey to extend the height of Lendal Tower and convert the building into a water tower. Water was pumped up to a cistern on the roof and from there, a piped water supply for the city was constructed using hollowed-out tree trunks. The company moved the pumping station upstream in 1846 but retained the use of the building. It is still used today as the offices of the York Waterworks plc.

Lendal Tower, seen here above Lendal Bridge, looks out over the River Ouse. One of the city's medieval defence sites, it was built, along with the tower on the opposite bank, to guard any approach, by water, from the north of the city.

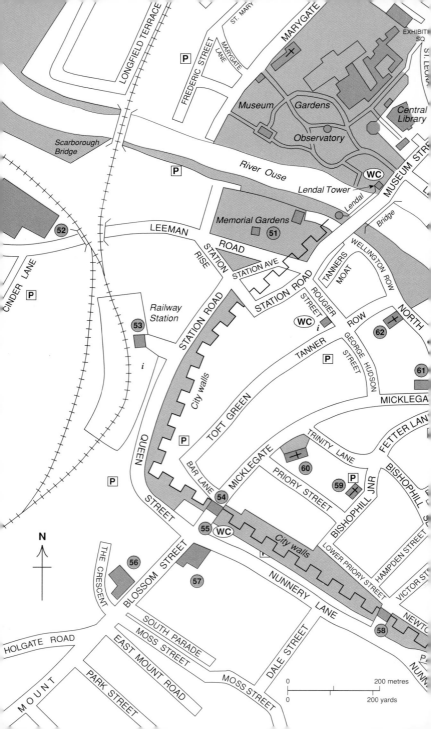

WEST OF THE RIVER OUSE

At sometime during their stay, most visitors will find that they will cross one or more of York's three road bridges to reach the attractions which lie west of the River Ouse.

York played a vital role in the railway history of this country and it is appropriate that the city is host to Britain's National Railway Museum. The nostalgia of steam vies with the latest technological innovations of rail travel among a host of displays. At a different end of the scale is the fascinating world of model railways in the York Model Railway exhibition.

This part of York also has three notable churches and an arts centre as well as the Bar Convent Museum and the impressive Micklegate Bar, sometimes referred to as the Royal Gateway. It was the most important of the four main, medieval gateways into the city.

51 **Memorial Gardens** (Leeman Road): A small area of peaceful parkland open to the public, between Leeman Road and the River Ouse, which commemorates those who fell in the two World Wars.

52 **National Railway Museum** (Leeman Road): Two hundred years of railway history are on display. Visitors can travel back to the

York's railway station, opened in 1877, is a fine example of Victorian architecture. The graceful curving roof mirrors the gentle sweep of the mainline tracks.

heyday of steam locomotion or appreciate the latest technology involved in the high speed travel of trains across the countryside of Britain and through the Channel Tunnel into Europe. There are some beautifully restored locomotives, powered by steam, diesel and electric and some of the great names in railway locomotion are on view: a reproduction of the Rocket (1829) launched upon the world at a speed of 29 miles per hour (46.6 kmh) by the inventive brilliance of George Stephenson (1781-1848) and the mighty Mallard which in 1938 set up the still-unbroken world speed record for a steam locomotive at 126 miles per hour (202.8 kmh).

The last name in luxury was provided for the members of Britain's royal family when they travelled by train and a model of Queen Victoria can be seen in her 'palace on wheels'. There are two railway exhibition halls, full of interest and exhibits with model railway, picture gallery, audio-visual shows and an ever-changing programme of special events and exhibitions.

York Model Railway (Tea Room Square, ㊾ York Station): A world in miniature with 5000 trees, 2500 people, 2000 lights, 1000 vehicles, and 600 buildings – a fascinating visual experience where up to 14 trains are running at any one time. The high speed Intercity train travels an amazing 14 miles (22.5 km) every day, as well as modern diesel, freight, overhead electric and occasionally the Orient Express and Royal Train. Adults and children alike will be absorbed by the lineside models and stations displayed in the beautifully preserved Hornby 3-rail layout. Thomas the Tank engine has his own display and time flies by from noon to night in a Bavarian town where a dramatic change in lighting takes place every three minutes.

Micklegate: Leads out of the city centre from the Ouse Bridge to Micklegate Bar. Joseph Hansom, a distinguished York architect who is chiefly remembered for his invention of the one-horse Hansom cab, was born at No. 114 in 1803.

54 **Micklegate Bar:** This is the most important

of the four main, medieval gateways into York and is sometimes referred to as the Royal Gateway. The route from London entered the city at this point and almost every English and British monarch (from 1066-1900) has ridden in ceremony through its medieval portals, except Henry VIII, who entered through Walmgate Bar (see p.69).

Apart from the pageantry, the battlements of Micklegate Bar were used for a more barbarous custom. The decapitated heads of criminals, traitors, rebels and enemies were boiled or pickled then fixed onto spiked poles which were then displayed on the gateway as a warning to others. Although the iron sockets to secure the poles are still to be seen, no heads have been displayed here since 1745.

Micklegate Bar - the three small figures at the top date from 1950, and are replacements of earlier statues which had eroded over time.

Micklegate Bar became a favourite place at which to pour public disgrace upon convicted enemies of the common law, the established religion and the crown. In the early 15th century, the Percys were among the most powerful and popular families in Yorkshire and Northumberland. However, Sir Henry Percy, known as Harry Hotspur because of his great speed in riding horses, rebelled against King Henry IV and their armies met at Shrewsbury in 1403. Harry Hostspur was killed in the battle and, as a warning to all Yorkshiremen, his head was sent to York to be spiked on Micklegate Bar.

Perhaps the most famous head on Micklegate Bar was that of Richard Plantagnet who was made Duke of York in 1415. In a rival claim for the throne, Richard waged war against Henry VI and in a St Albans street battle in May 1455 the Yorkist troops of Richard devasted the Lancastrian soldiers of the King. (This began the 30-year campaign between the Houses of York and Lancaster in which the throne changed hands five times and was not finally settled until Henry VII married Elizabeth of York in 1486). Richard was killed at Wakefield in 1460 by royalist soldiers who cut off his head and took it to York and placed it on Micklegate Bar for all to see. 'Off with his head, and set it on York gates; So York may overlook the town of York' says Henry's Queen Margaret in Shakespeare's *Henry VI Part III*.

The cause of the northern Catholics was championed in the 16th century by Sir Thomas Percy, 7th Earl of Northumberland. One of the leaders of the rebellion against the Protestant Queen Elizabeth, the Earl was captured and beheaded in public at Parliament Street in York. Although his head was spiked on Micklegate Bar, it disappeared one night. In response to a reward of ten shillings and six pence, the grisly remains were recovered from a grave in Holy Trinity Church, Goodramgate and returned to the spike. Small wonder that his headless phantom haunts Holy Trinity churchyard, still searching for his head!

The base and outer portals of the bar were built in stone in the 12th century and the upper structure was added about 1332. Only the main arch is medieval, the pedestrian arch is 18th century and the other two side arches were constructed in the 19th century to ease the flow of traffic. Micklegate Bar originally had a barbican (extension archway with second gateway) but it was demolished in 1826.

35 **Micklegate Bar Museum** (Micklegate Bar): A small museum is housed within the bar and gives an insight into York's civil and social history.

36 **Odeon Cinema** (Blossom Street): A three-screen cinema. The building is typical of the cinema era of the 1930s and is a Listed Building of architectural interest.

37 **Bar Convent Museum** (Blossom Street): A fine Georgian building built in the 1760s, with no clue as to the beautiful Catholic chapel that lies within. This was deliberate. At that time, Catholic chapels were still illegal and the nuns of the Institute of the Blessed Virgin Mary (founded 1686) decided to conceal their place of worship, built in 1769, from outside observers. Religious persecution explains the provision of nine exits in the chapel for quick escapes and a priest's hiding hole under the chapel floor. The museum takes a pilgrimage through 300

The clock above the entrance to the Bar Convent Museum. Due to religious persecution, the architect of the Bar Convent was instructed to disguise the existence of a Roman Catholic Chapel inside, which dates from 1769.

years of Christian history in the north of England, along with the story of Mary Ward, foundress of the Institute.

Victoria Bar (Victor Street)): This 19th- 58 century archway was built to achieve a way through the medieval city wall and give access for traffic between Bishophill (inside the walls) and Nunnery Lane. It was constructed in 1838 and named after Queen Victoria (1837-1901).

St Mary's Church (Bishophill Junior): 59 Dating back to the 10th century, the ancient square tower is the oldest church tower in York. The tower itself is built with stone from the remains of a Roman building and an Anglo-Saxon cross is preserved inside the church. The interior dates from the 11th to the 15th century.

Holy Trinity Church (Micklegate): This 60 belonged to the Holy Trinity Priory (1089-1426) run by the Benedictine order. Only a small fragment of the medieval priory church remains and part of the original church's central tower can be seen near the chancel steps. It was here, outside the gateway (demolished in 1856) of the priory, that the medieval Mystery Plays began their street-tour performance.

The Mystery Plays developed from the dramatisation of biblical scenes which were performed by the clergy in order to enliven normal church services. These began in the 13th century and their popularity spread to plays which were organised in the large towns and cities by the craft guilds (a guild was a type of medieval trade union). The name given to the plays derived from the skill acquired by an apprentice which was called 'the mystery'. Records of the York Cycle of Mystery Plays date from 1340 and each guild had a wagon on which they enacted a biblical story, often appropriate to their guild – the Shipwrights for example would perform the the Building of the Ark. Up to 40 pageant wagons would begin at the gate of Holy Trinity Church, Micklegate and then proceed to each of the other 11 playing sites, where the plays would be presented to the street audience. The plays, discontinued in the 16th century when the Puritans decreed that the theatre was immoral, were revived in 1951 and are now performed every four years, the next will be in the year 2000.

(31) York Arts Centre (Micklegate): Converted from the former St John the Evangelist church, this is a centre for the performing arts with a programme of drama, music, poetry, dance and films.

(32) All Saints' Church (North Street): Between Ouse Bridge and Lendal Bridge, the slender tower of All Saints' provides a notable landmark. Here is one of York's fine medieval churches which is particularly noted for its wealth of 15th-century glass painting and a carved roof. A window in the north aisle is called the 'Pricke of Conscience'; it depicts scenes from the end of the world and includes some fairly awesome events. Among a group of 15th-century angels on the lower right-hand panel in the south aisle window, is one who wears a pair of spectacles – they were invented in the 12th century!

The city of York has one of the world's finest collections of medieval stained glass. This window can be seen in All Saints' Church, North Street.

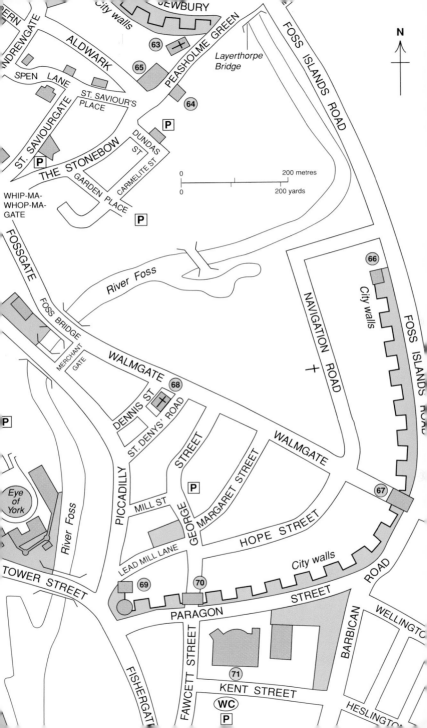

EAST & SOUTH-EAST OF THE CITY

Straddling a wide bend in the River Foss, the east and south-east parts of the city are bounded by a substantial section of the medieval city walls. Walmgate Bar, complete with its barbican, is the most notable feature along this part of the walls.

Historical interests in this part of the city include a half-timbered pub, a medieval guildhall and two medieval churches, one of which is the second oldest in York. Just outside the city walls is the Barbican Centre, housing important entertainment, sport and leisure facilities.

㉒ **St Cuthbert's Church** (Peasholme Green): Dating from the 17th century, this is York's second oldest church (the first being York Minster) and has stones from a Roman building incorporated into the walls. There is an inscription in the church relating to General James Wolfe who died in the hour of victory at the Siege of Quebec in 1759. The church is now the administrative centre for St Michael le Belfrey church.

㉔ **Black Swan** (Peasholme Green): This is a historic, half-timbered public house with a unique atmosphere, gained from a mixture of styles which span the centuries. Although the features date mainly from the 17th century, the story of the Black Swan begins back in the 15th century when a house was built on the site by a city merchant, William Bowes. Some of the present timber probably dates from this early period. William was a distinguished citizen of the city and twice became Lord Mayor of York (1417 and 1428). His son, William, also became Lord Mayor in 1443; his grandson, Martin, born here in 1497, left home for London at the age of 14 and eventually became Lord Mayor of London, Treasurer to the Royal Mint in the reign of Queen Elizabeth I, and was knighted. Sir Martin Bowes presented a Sword of State to his home city and it remains as one of York's treasures.

In the latter quarter of the 17th century, the manor house belonged to the Thompson family. The fireplaces, doorways, a staircase and oak panelling, date from this period. Henrietta

York Minster from the Bar Walls near Layerthorpe Bridge.

Thompson, who was born here, married Colonel Edward Wolfe of Westerham, Kent where their son James (1727-59) was born. At the side of Black Swan there is an inscription which states that James Wolfe was baptised in the small ancient church called St Clements which existed here at that time. It is known to the locals as 'The Birthplace of Canada' because it was James, as General James Wolfe of the British Army, who commanded the defeat of the French during the 12-week Siege of Quebec (1759). He died from his wounds in the hour of victory.

Adding further intrigue at this unique public house is a secret room that was probably used for cock fighting, and a secret passage, previously used during time of religious persecution, which links the inn with St Cuthbert's Church opposite.

65 **St Anthony's Hall** (Peasholme Green): One of the three surviving medieval guildhalls in York, now occupied by the Borthwick Institute of Historical Research, part of York University.

66 **Red Tower** (Foss Islands Road): Built as a watchtower in 1490, its name refers to the colour of the bricks which were used to construct the building on stone foundations. Resentment by the stonemasons against the use of bricks culminated in the murder of one of the tilers or bricklayers. At the side of the Tower you can see the projecting garderobe (lavatory).

67 **Walmgate Bar:** A magnificent gateway, complete with its barbican (the only complete medieval city barbican in England). At the top of the 12th-century archway you can see the projecting spikes of the portcullis. Massive oak

Walmgate Bar. Built in the manner of a medieval castle entrance, the four main gateways in York each had a barbican (an extension archway with another gateway). Only Walmgate Bar has survived complete with its barbican.

69

doors dating from the 15th century, still in place, presented a formidable barrier but pedestrians could gain access via the small wicket gate set in the door.

Against the inner city side of Walmgate Bar is a house of wood and plaster. It was added during the second half of the 16th century and occupied by the gatekeeper. After being badly damaged during the English Civil War (the Siege of York took place in 1644), Walmgate Bar was restored with stone from the nearby ruins of a church destroyed in the Siege.

Foss Islands Road: This road takes its name from the marshy islands which started to form here during the 17th century, due to the silting up of the huge medieval lake referred to as the King's Pool, the King's Fish Pool or the Fishpond of the Foss. When a new bed for the river was channelled in 1792, the islands dried out and later, Foss Islands Road was built alongside part of the river bank.

St Denys' Church (Walmgate): Originally 68 twice its present size, the nave was dismantled in 1798 and a new doorway created with the Norman porch. In the north aisle of this fine medieval church are two colourful medallions of early 13th-century glass, examples of some of the oldest glass in the city.

Fishergate Postern (Fishergate): In addi- 69 tion to the four main gateways (bars) into the city there were six lesser gateways called posterns which also had a tower. The Fishergate Postern is the narrow pointed archway and although the portcullis is no longer there, the grooves and the crook hinges can still be seen. At the side of the gateway is Fishergate Postern Tower, the only one of the six postern towers which has remained unaltered and has a garderobe (lavatory) affixed to its side.

Fishergate Bar (Paragon Street): This is the 70

location of one of the six lesser gateways (posterns) built in the 14th century, but the present gateway with its wide central arch and two flanking passages dates from the early 15th century. On the underside of the archway you can see the burn marks that were caused by a fire in 1489 when riots against taxation took place and the gateway was badly damaged. Instead of a repair, the gateway was

blocked by bricks and remained so for over 300 years until it was re-opened in 1827.

(71) **York Barbican Centre** (Barbican Road): One of the region's major centres for entertainment, sport and leisure facilities. An auditorium seats 1500 and is host to touring shows and artists in the world of entertainment including comedy, classical music, jazz, pop, rock and variety acts. Visitors are welcome to use the sports facilities including two swimming pools, sauna, solarium, indoor climbing wall and fitness studio. In the main sports hall are facilities for badminton, basketball, fencing, five-a-side football, netball and volleyball.

Fishergate Bar, which was burnt and badly damaged by rioters in 1489. Scorch and fire marks can still be seen under the central arch.

INFORMATION DIRECTORY

PLEASE NOTE:
(1) Addresses: all addresses are York, unless otherwise stated.
(2) Telephone: When telephoning from within the city of York, omit the national code 01904 from all numbers.
(3) Information Enquiries: see list of Tourist Information Centres (TICs) in York for all enquiries.
(4) Information is believed to be correct at the time of publication but names and telephone numbers may be subject to change.

ACCOMMODATION
A list of **Hotels, Guest Houses & Self-Catering Accommodation** is published in the 'York Visitor Guide' which is available free of charge from the York TICs.

Youth & Group Accommodation
New Racecourse Centre
Dringhouses, YO2 2QG
Tel: 01904 636553

York International Youth Hostel
Haverford, Water End, Clifton,
YO3 6LT
Tel: 01904 653147

York Youth Hotel
Bishophill House,
11/13 Bishophill Senior,YO1 1EF
Tel: 01904 625904 / 630613

Caravan and Camping Sites
The following sites have 60 or more pitches.

Cawood Caravan and Camping Centre,
Ryther Road, Cawood, Selby,
YO8 0TT
Tel: 01757 268450

Mount Pleasant Caravan Village,
Acaster Malbis, YO2 1UW
Tel:01904 707078

Poplar Farm Caravan Park
Acaster Malbis, Y02 1UH
Tel: 01759 371377

Weir Caravan Park
Stamford Bridge, York Y04 1AN
Tel: 01759 371377

ACTIVITIES FOR CHILDREN
(See MUSEUMS AND SPORTS)

AIRPORTS
(see TRAVEL)

ART GALLERIES
(See MUSEUMS)

BANKS / BUREAUX DE CHANGE

Banks
Most of the banks in the city provide exchange facilities.
Normal banking hours are:
9.30-17.00 Mon-Fri
9.30-12.00 / 15.00 Sat.

Bureaux de Change
American Express
6 Stonegate
Tel: 01904 611727
Mon-Fri: 9.00-17.30
Sat: 9.00-17.00
Sun: April-Oct, 10.30-4.30

Thomas Cook Travel
Nessgate
Tel: 01904 653626
Mon-Sat: 9.00-17.30
Thurs: 9.00-10.00

Also at 31 Stonegate
Tel: 01904 644344

Tourist Information Centre,
De Grey Rooms, Exhibition Square
Tel: 01904 621756
Mon-Sun: 9.00-4.00. Buy only

Tourist Information Centre,
Railway Station
Tel: 01904 621756
Mon-Sun: 9.00-4.00. Buy only

York Tourism Bureau,
6 Rougier Street
Tel: 01904 620557
Mon-Sat; April-Oct, 9.00-18.00
Sun: April-Oct, 10.00-16.00
Mon-Sat: Nov-Mar, 9.00-17.00
Buy only

CAR HIRE
Avis. Tel: 01904 610460
Ford Rent-a-Car. Tel: 01904 615008
Vauxhall Rental. Tel: 01904 625444
Also listed in Yellow Pages.

CAR PARKS
Car parks are located on the street
maps in this Pocket Guide.
A Park & Ride service is available
from three car parks at the edges of
the city. On driving into the city,
follow the signs (P+bus) for
(1) Askham Bar (2) Clifton Moor
(3) Grimston Bar car parks.
Enquiries Tel: 01904 431388 /
707726

CHURCHES
(See PLACES OF WORSHIP)

CINEMAS
Odeon Cinema
Blossom St, YO2 2AJ
Tel: 01904 623040 (see p.63)

Warner Cinemas
Clifton Moor Centre
Clifton Moor, YO3 4XY
Tel: 01904 691199

CYCLE HIRE, CYCLEWAYS
A cycleways map is available from
the TICs.

Bob Trotter Cycle Shop
Tel: 01904 622868

York Cycleworks
Tel: 01904 626664

DISABLED, Facilities for
A leaflet is available from the
TICs.

EMERGENCIES
Phone 999 for Fire, Police or
Ambulance

EXHIBITIONS
(see MUSEUMS)

FESTIVALS & EVENTS
A list of festivals and events
is published in the York Visitor
Guide, available free from the TICs.
Major festivals include:

(1) Jorvik Viking Festival (Feb)
Tel: 01904 653000 / 643211;

(2) York Early Music Festival (July)
Tel: 01904 645738;

(3) York Cycle of Mystery Plays
(every four years). York Theatre
Royal, Tel: 01904 623568

GHOST TRAILS
(See WALKS)

LIBRARIES
Central Library
Museum Street
Tel: 01904 655631.

LOST PROPERTY
(see POLICE)

MEDICAL SERVICES
(1) For ordinary illness or minor acci-
dent, ask your hotel or place of residence for details of a local doctor,
dentist or late-night chemist.
(2) For Emergencies: Phone 999 for
Fire, Police or Ambulance.
(3) York District Hospital
Wigginton Road, Tel: 01904 631313

MUSEUMS, ART GALLERIES & EXHIBITIONS

The ARC,
St Saviourgate, YO1 2NN
Tel: 01904 654324 (see p.34)

Bar Convent Museum,
Blossom Street
Tel: 01904 643238 (see p.63)

Barley Hall,
Coffee Yard, Swinegate
(see p.40)

Bedern Hall,
Bedern
Tel: 01904 625401 (see p.25)

Fairfax House,
Castlegate, YO1 1RN
Te: 01904 655543 (see p.47)

Friargate Wax Museum,
Lower Friargate, YO1 1SL
Tel: 01904 658775 (see p.43)

Impressions Gallery,
29 Castlegate, YO1 1RN
Tel: 01904 654724 (see p.49)

Jorvik Viking Centre,
Coppergate, YO1 1NT
Tel: 01904 643211 (see p.49)

Merchant Adventurer's Hall,
Fossgate, YO1 2XD
Tel: 01904 654818 (see p.32)

Merchant Taylors' Hall
Aldwark, YO1 2BX
Tel: 01904 632967 (see p.25)

Micklegate Bar Museum,
Micklegate Bar, YO1 1JX
Tel: 01904 634436 (see p.63)

National Railway Museum,
Leeman Road, Y02 4XJ
Tel: 01904 621261 (see p.59)

Regimental Museum,
Tower St. YO1 1SB
Tel: 01904 662790 (see p.46)

Richard III Museum,
Monk Bar, YO1 2LH
Tel: 01904 634191 (see p.25)

St Anthony's Hall,
Borthwick Institute,
Peasholme Green
Tel: 01904 642315 (see p.69)

St. William's College,
College Street, YO1 2JF
Tel: 01904 637134 (see p.22)

Treasurer's House,
Minster Yard, YO1 2JD
Tel: 01904 624247 (see p.20)

York Arts Centre,
Micklegate,YO11JG
Tel: 01904 627129 (see p.65)

York Castle Museum,
Eye of York, YO1 1RY
Tel: 01904 653611 (see p.44)

York City Art Gallery,
Exhibition Square, YO1 2EW
Tel: 01904 551861 (see p.51)

York Dungeon,
12 Clifford Street, YO1 1RD
Tel: 01904 632599 (see p.43)

York Minster,
Deangate, YO1 2JA
Tel: 01904 624426 (see p17)

York Model Railway,
Tearoom Square, York Station, YO2 2AB
Tel 01904 630169 (see p.60)

York Story
Castlegate YO1 1RN
Tel: 01904 628632 (see p.49)

Yorkshire Museum,
Museum Gardens, YO1 2DR
Tel: 01904 629745 (see p.54)

Yorvik Brass-Rubbing Centre,
57 Skeldergate, YO1 1DS
Tel: 01904 630456 (see p.44)

NIGHT CLUBS
Silks
12 Clifford Street,
Tel: 01904 647947

Toff's Nightclub & Restaurant
3-5 Toft Green
Tel: 01904 620603

Ziggy's Nightclub
53/55 Micklegate
Tel: 01904 620602
Tel: 01904 620674

PLACES OF WORSHIP
(City centre locations)

Church of England
York Minster
Deangate
Tel: 01904 624426
and 01904 622943 (24 hours)

St Michael le Belfrey Church
Low Petergate
Tel: 01904 624190

St Helen's Church
Davygate
Tel: 01904 625186

St Denys' Church
Walmgate
Tel: 01904 631116

All Saints' Church
Pavement
Tel: 01904 631116

Methodist Church
Trinity Methodist Church
Monkgate
Tel: 01904 761711

Central Methodist Church
St Saviourgate
Tel: 01904 426483

Roman Catholic
St Wilfrid's Church
Duncombe Place
Tel: 01904 624767

Society of Friends
Friends' Meeting House
Clifford Street
Tel: 01904 624065

POLICE
North Yorkshire Police
Fulford Road, Y01 4BY
Tel: 01904 631321
Ask for Help Desk.

PUBLIC HOUSES & WINE BARS
(Within the City Walls)

* Most public houses have under-gone alterations and refurbishments over the years, including the recreation of earlier styles. The public houses marked with an asterisk are noted for the preservation, to varying degrees, of their original layout and period interiors. They date in the main from the 19th and early 20th centuries and reveal examples of authentic Victorian and Edwardian styles. Some of the features in the Black Swan in Peasholme Green date back to the 17th century.

Ackhorne Inn
9 St Martins Lane
Tel: 01904 629820

Black Swan*
23 Peasholme Green
Tel: 01904 625236

Blue Bell*
53 Fossgate
Tel: 01904 654904

Bonding Warehouse
Skeldergate
Tel: 01904 622527

Brewers Arms
Tanner Row
Tel: 01904 638486

Corner Pin
Tanner Row
Tel: 01904 629946

Cross Keys
Goodramgate
Tel: 01904 610866

Falcon The,*
94 Micklegate
Tel: 01904 622225

Golden Slipper
20 Goodramgate
Tel: 01904 651235

Hole in the Wall
High Petergate
Tel: 01904 634468

Kings Arms
Kings Staithes
Tel: 01904 659435

Lowther The,
Cumberland Street
Tel: 01904 622987

McMillans Cafe Bar
1 Rougier Street
Tel: 01904 625438

Maltings The,
Tanners Moat
Tel: 01904 655387

Nags Head
Micklegate
Tel: 01904 659019

Northern Wall The,
5 Fossgate
Tel: 01904 610293

Old White Swan
Goodramgate
Tel: 01904 622463

Phoenix The,*
75 George Street
Tel: 01904 652594

Plonkers Wine Bar
5 Cumberland Street
Tel: 01904 655307

Punch Bowl Inn
7 Stonegate
Tel: 01904 622305

Punch Bowl Hotel
Blossom Street
Tel: 10904 622619

Railway King Hotel
George Hudson Street
Tel: 01904 645161

Royal Oak*
18 Goodramgate
Tel: 01904 653856S

Tap & Spile
29 Monkgate
Tel: 01904 656158

Three Tuns
Coppergate
Tel: 01904 621873

Yates's Wine Lodge
Church Lane
Tel: 01904 613569

York Arms*
26 High Petergate
Tel: 01904 624508

Youngs Hotel
25 High Petergate
Tel: 01904 671001

RACECOURSE
York Racecourse
Knavesmire Road
Tel: 01904 620911

RESTAURANTS
York has a wealth of restaurants offering an opportunity to sample a range of international cuisine as well as traditional British cooking. A list of restaurants is available from the TICs.

SHOPPING
Many of the streets in the centre of York are traffic-free during the middle of the day but visitors should

always check before crossing the roads. A vast array of shops selling a large range of fascinating items makes shopping and browsing through the network of ancient and modern streets an experience of delight and discovery. World-famous streets of the Shambles and Stonegate are thronged with pedestrians in the summer but a diversion into some side streets and alleyways such as Grape Lane, Little Stonegate and Coffee Yard will lead to a variety of intriguing shops with specialised goods. Within the thriving city centre there is an abundant choice of shops, including the most modern of department stores, and the main shopping streets are Coney Street and Parliament Street.

SPORTS AND LEISURE FACILITIES

Further information on sport and leisure activities is available from city of York Leisure Services, Tel: 01904 613161

Indoor Centres

Barbican Centre,
Barbican Road, YO1 4NT
Tel: 01904 630266 (Sports Desk)
Clifton Park Sports Complex
Shipton Road, Clifton
Tel: 01904 623602

Oaklands Sports Centre,
Cornlands Road.
Tel: 01904 782841

Sports Centre & Stadium,
Jockey Lane, Huntington
Tel: 01904 613310 / 613313

Swimming Pools

Barbican Centre,
Barbican Road
Tel: 01904 630266

Edmund Wilson Pool,
Thanet Rd, Acomb,
Tel: 01904 793031

Yearsley Pool
Hayleys Terrace,
Tel: 01904 622773

Leisure Pool Centre,
Jockey Lane, Huntington
Tel: 01904 613310 / 613313

Golf Clubs

Aldwark Manor, Tel: 01347 838353
Forest Park, Tel: 01904 400688
Fulford, Tel: 01904 413579
Heworth,Tel: 01904 424618
Pike Hills,Tel: 01904 706566
York, Tel: 01904 490304
York Centre, Tel: 01904 470549

Bowling Greens (public)

Barbican Centre; Clarence Gardens; Exhibition; Glen Gardens; Hull Road Park; Museum Gardens; Rowntree Park; Scarcroft; West Park

Ten-Pin-Bowling

Gx Superbowl
Jockey Lane, Huntington,
Tel: 01904 656595

Megabowl
Clifton Moor
Tel: 01904 690006

TOILETS

Bootham Bar; Coppergate; Kent Street car park; Monk Bar; Museum Gardens; Nunnery Lane car park; Parliament Street; St George's Field car park; Tanner Row; Union Terrace car park.

TOURIST INFORMATION CENTRES

Guide Friday
De Grey Rooms
Exhibition Square, YO1 2HB
Tel: 01904 621756

Guide Friday
Railway Station
Tel: 01904 621756

York Tourism Bureau
6 Rougier Street, YO1 1JA
Tel: 01904 620557

THEATRES, CONCERT HALLS
(Box office phone numbers)

Grand Opera House
Cumberland Street, YO1 1SW
Tel: 01904 671818

Theatre Royal
St Leonard's Place, YO1 2HD
Tel: 01904 623568

York Barbican Centre
Barbican Road, YO1 4NT
Tel: 01904 656688

TRAVEL & TOURS

Air
(York is about one hour's drive
from the nearest airport).
Leeds Bradford Airport
Tel: 0113 250 9696

Manchester Airport
(direct train to York)
Tel: 0161 489 3000

Bus & Coach
National Express
(Coach services to York from
most parts of Britain)
Tel: 0990 80808

Rider York
(Local bus operator)
Tel: 01904 624161

City Tours
A number of companies operate
regular open-topped bus tours of
the city. Horse-drawn carriage tours
operate from Duncombe Place.

Rail
York Railway Station
Tel: 0345 484950
(British Rail train enquiries)

River Cruise
Castle Line	Tel: 0113 2438561
Star Line	Tel: 01757 248764
White Rose Line	Tel: 01904 628324
York Marine	Tel: 01904 704442

Sea
(York is about one hour's drive from
Hull docks).
North Sea Ferries
Tel: 01482 795141

Taxis
Taxi ranks at the Railway Station and
Duncombe Place. Some of the taxi
companies in Yellow Pages include:

Ace	Tel: 01904 638888
ABC Blue Circle	Tel: 01904 638787
A Team	Tel: 01904 643111
Fleetways	Tel: 01904 645333
Streamline	Tel: 01904 638833

WALKS

Guided tours around the city are
very popular and are organised by
several companies. A Walkman set
and tapes are also available for hire
with a choice of two itineraries.

Ghost walks provide some chilling
tales on an evening's stroll through
the haunted city.

Short Walks. There are pleasant
walks through the Museum
Gardens, Dean's Park and along the
riverside.

City Walls. The short section
between Bootham Bar and Monk
Bar should not be missed. A
complete circuit of the Bar Walls
will take up to two hours.

BOOK LIST
Beal, Pauline *Walking the Walls*
1994
Dunn-Smith, Neville *Walk Through
York* 1986
Jones, Mark W *A Walk around the
Snickelways of York* 1993
Matthews, Rupert *Haunted York*
1992
Pitkin Guide, *City of York* 1995
Ramm, Herman *Roman York from
AD71* 1991
Yorkshire Evening Press *York Guide*
1996

INDEX